Lights, Cubicle, Actio

100+ Directives for Survival in Corporate Am

M000032111

All Rights Reserved

ISBN: 0-9708728-0-1

Lights, Cubicle, Action! copyright © 2003 by The DocVoc® Press. All rights reserved. This book was manufactured in the United States of America. No part of this book, its cover or contents, may be reproduced in any manner, except for purposes of editorial review. For further copies of this publication or related materials in the series contact The DocVoc® Press, P.O. Box 2458, Reston, Virginia 20195 or visit www.docvoc.com.

ISBN: 0-9708728-0-1
Bookland EAN: 9-780970-872807

First Printing December 2002

DocVoc® is a Trademark of DocVoc® Enterprises all rights reserved

For Businesses and Academic Institutions
Copies of this material are available with discounts for bulk purchases. To obtain additional copies of this publication contact
The DocVoc® Press, P.O. Box 2458, Reston, Virginia 20195 or visit www.docvoc.com.
For additional copies of *Lights, Cubicle, Action!*, call 1-800-345-6665, fax: 603-357-2073, or email: orders@pathwaybook.com.
For questions related to *Lights, Cubicle, Action!*, or other DocVoc Press publications email: books@docvoc.com

Preface

Lights, Cubicle, Action! began as a way of uncharacteristically capturing the dubious corporate rhetoric that at one time or another has spotlighted each of us. In business as in all walks of life we have come to believe so much propaganda about what really is and why it is when nothing could be further from our truth. In fact, even our truth is often situational. While other inspirational and self-help works shoot their typical charge of motivation through your veins *Lights, Cubicle, Action!* grips you uniquely. Through *Lights* "anti-quotes" you'll see the glossy ideology of corporate life stripped clean leaving you at center stage with the edge to see business more clearly.

The journey to capture these anti-quotes began nearly twenty years ago and still continues today. Compiled through teaching, listening, climbing ladders, falling off ladders, and building new ladders, these humorous yet piercing and provocative quips were assembled to combat and debunk myths from the entire corporate spectrum. *Lights* rips through the malaise of corporate-speak and grants you the perspective most of us share but rarely discuss. With *Lights* in hand you'll beg to discuss these poignant proclamations. Here are some of my personal favorites:

> *When you wait for your promotion what you are really saying is "Take control of my life."*
>
> *Everybody works hard.....just ask them!*
>
> *He who lies first is most believed.*
>
> *"Good idea" means "I should have thought of that."*

So sit back laugh, scream, shake your head, and share these insights with everyone you know who feels the same way as you.

a.a.cantor
December 2002

This book is dedicated to every worker who wonders why and how things happen in the workplace.
Americans live to work. We should at least understand how WORK works.

Acknowledgements

I wish to thank the following individuals without whose help this publication would not have evolved. To Inga Schiedemandel for her tireless editing efforts, Jed Dinger and Ted Frymark for their keen production insight and graphical inspiration and especially to Patti Gabany who kept me focused and supported me through this labor of love.

Lights, Cubicle, Action!

100+ Directives for Survival in Corporate America

Fiat Lux

(let there be light)

Contents

1

The self-made man is an absolutely wonderful fairy tale.

Every Mr. Allbymyself who succeeds at anything has had help, whether it was a customer willing to take a chance on his product or a mentor that steered him in the right direction. Whether it was someone willing to invest in his business or someone generous enough to help him complete the necessary tasks, every successful person has had help. We call people "self-made" because it suggests that each of us alone has the opportunity to go from rags to riches. But the only way to make it alone is to start alone, be alone, and stay alone. One who experiences this solitude would more likely fade into obscurity than emerge as a fantastic and promotable icon.

2

When you succeed at a job you don't want, like, or deem considerable, you have failed.

So often we do what we think others want us to do. And we do it so well that others are happy with our results. But what about what we want? Don't our desires about how we spend our time matter? Maybe we fear the change of income, location, or responsibilities, rarely if ever asking ourselves, "Do I quit by leaving or do I quit by staying?" I say one quits by staying, unless one has a vocation that one: 1) can really live with, 2) will not resent, and 3) will not look back upon someday and lament all that one missed by staying. If staying is right then the follow-up question is, "Why can't what I'd lose by leaving be gotten somewhere else in another form or fashion?" People all over the world are making millions of dollars and taking almost complete control of their time by doing some of the most unimaginable things like managing scrap yards or teaching others how to sleep.

~3~

One person in a group of a thousand can be the only one who's right.

Democracy is a wonderful way to come to consensus about an issue but speaks only to what is most popular or most agreed to and not necessarily what's right. History is littered with examples of popular ideas that were later proved incorrect by one or very few individuals. One who combats a thousand in an idea rarely emerges victorious because of the sheer enormity of braving the wave of opposition. That strong opposition often swallows Mr. Contrarian, who, like the pioneers of old, ends up with an arrow in his back. Too often we determine later that Mr. Contrarian actually was correct. Be glad that for the most part we're no longer executed for being contrarians.

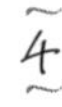

Employees and businesses choose to endure each other.

The equation of employment is quite simple. It is made up of three items: *You*, *Employer*, and *Fit*. *You* are the proprietor of some marketable skill or ability (i.e., your shtick). *Employer* is the business entity considering whether your shtick is actually worth having around the office. If Employer decides that You are worth having and You decide that Employer is worth taking money from for an undisclosed period of time, two choices are made: 1) You choose to endure the work and pay provided by Employer and 2) Employer chooses to endure bringing You onboard. The business-lingo term for this mysterious covalent bond is *Fit*. At the heart of Fit is a mutual choice of endurance.

~
5
~

Most people who worry about being fired are never in danger of being fired.

Employees enter jobs with all sorts of mindsets: superiority complexes, inferiority complexes, and righteous indignation to name a few. While one works with those mindsets toward success, first one must survive. There is a certain level of humility one has when one worries about being fired. With survival threatened one is likely to demonstrate superior dedication, attention to detail, and a willingness to succeed as an incumbent. Through those invigorating qualities one often exhibits behavior not before seen or imagined. And those exhibitions help one keep a job more often than one loses it.

~6~

One of the most gratifying experiences one can have is showing someone how they were wrong.

There is great fulfillment in knowing the answer to something someone else did not. Being able to demonstrate that knowledge is a way, no matter how humbly presented, of showing superiority. Ms. Righteous might seem ugly gaining pleasure in showing her superiority at yours or someone else's expense, but that ugliness can always be downplayed by her curt smile or brief "I'm sorry." What isn't ugly is how much better Ms. Righteous feels from her renewed self-confidence.

7

The overwhelming difference in two careers is the materials one chooses to read.

Accumulation of knowledge builds the foundation of excellence in any profession. People in different careers invariably know different things. No matter what people do for a living, it is fairly certain that their career path toward where they are today has involved a considerable amount of reading, whether it was manuals, charts, maps, or novels. Educational systems are set up to give people the opportunity to choose learning materials to propel them along a path, and the professional world exaggerates these opportunities. Were we to begin again and move along a different career path, we would have read different materials simply because our positions would have dictated so. Therefore, had we wanted a different career, we should have read differently.

~ 8 ~

The quicker you fire someone, the sooner they can find the job that most satisfies them.

Employees shouldn't be kept in jobs one moment past discovering they are not doing their jobs effectively. Sure, we can rationalize that with a few minor adjustments the poor performer will improve and eventually emerge as a great performer. This works sometimes but not most of the time. Why? These employees, however much we want them to be, are simply not a good fit. By firing these employees, we put them in a position to find jobs much more suited to their abilities, tastes, and desires. We have helped them. Conversely, by keeping them in their jobs, we stunt their growth and do a disservice to company's overall objectives.

Most people get up in the morning and go to work because they don't have the guts to go somewhere else.

If 10 million dollars were dropped in one's lap today, there is a good chance the only reason one would go to work the next day, in a new black Porsche, is to brag about one's newfound wealth. But on a typical day, one probably drives to work thinking about the hundred other places one would rather be driving, the places where stress is a little lighter, the pace is a little slower, one is a little happier. Still, one waits until Saturday, where one's ability to get up and get out in the car is so much easier, regardless of the time of day. That's okay. If one waits long enough and always eschews the risk of going somewhere other than work one will eventually retire then pass on. The lament will then pass too.

10

People want to work with people they want around them infinitely more than people who can get the job done.

Bosses hire people they like. Employees seek assignments with people they like. While both situations can produce effective results, the emotional relationship drives the employment relationship not the other way around. Only when the skill sets of two employees are so disparate that choosing the more-liked-but-less-skilled employee guarantees disaster will he not be chosen. This is rarely the case because disaster is mostly learned in hindsight, once the more likable employee is chosen. Seventy percent of all people hired into positions are hired through recommendations. And recommendations are what someone else, who liked the candidate, was willing to profess about the candidate.

11

All jobs are temp jobs.

No job is forever regardless of how entrenched an employee is. What is so permanent about permanent jobs? Hiring managers wave the "permanent" label over a candidate as if it was the cornucopia of employment. However, with the hallowed promise of perpetuity "permanent" is more like the burden of Sisyphus. Hiring managers should say, "This is a permanent job until you quit, we go out of business, or you are fired; all which will certainly take place long before you or we expect it to." The concept of permanent and temporary jobs was a myth created for the sole purpose of financial accounting through fair labor standards. Because some "temporary" assignments last five years and most permanent jobs don't the trick doesn't work anymore. Nearly all jobs can be done on contract, temporarily, and all permanent jobs will end.

12

Employees paid between $20,000 and $50,000 are the hardest workers, the most ingenious, the most diligent, the most loyal, the most stressed, and enjoy the fruits of their labor the least.

Many great ideas in companies come from people in the trenches; the worker-bees who manage to get their ideas escalated to the point where no one knows their true origin. These individuals mark their careers by staying later than most, compiling reports for managers just above them on the organizational charts, carrying the biggest burden of getting tasks completed, especially in the divisions of marketing and finance. These individuals are grateful just to be employed, but they are the toilers, and are rarely given their just rewards except in the form of token appreciations: a plaque, a modest bonus, or an extra slice of pizza at the corporate lunch. They sustain the business but reap little because 1) they do not focus on that fact they are the life-blood of the company, 2) they rarely unite to change the status quo and 3) they are easily replaceable.

13

The earth is simply one large exercise wheel for our rat race.

We scramble all over this country and the world alike, trying to find our way through our careers and our lives. As we ascend the corporate ladder, we are more than willing to eat plentifully from the cup of misfortune that has befallen our fellow rodents. Yet even in our ascension we mostly find our way simply by repeating the same predictable behavior. These behaviors include going to and from work along the habit-trails we call highways and performing repetitive tasks for the ultimate payment of cheese in the form of money.

14

Formal education is just an excuse to deny yourself your dreams.

Ask any degreed individual what their dream job is. Most will tell you something very different from what they do. Inevitably they'll rationalize their good job, good benefits, and livable salary. Is that really living? The trap of education is that most people feel compelled to do something related to what they've studied and never digress, even though that education had little to do with their dreams. Too much risk, too difficult. Except for doctors or lawyers, most people who live their dreams put little stock in their formal education. Instead these dreamers concentrate on their experiences and the acquisition of requisite knowledge, both which mostly occur outside the formal educational system.

15

There are no good jobs or bad jobs, only people who are happy in them and people who aren't.

Jobs by nature are neither good nor bad. They may be unpopular or difficult. They may be disliked by a lot of people or loved by nearly everyone. But these are merely feelings about the job and not the job itself. It is the matching or mismatching of one's desires to do a job with the responsibilities of that job that creates the notion of a good or bad job. When there is a match, it is more likely that an individual is happy doing the job. When there isn't a match, it is more likely that an individual is unhappy in the job. But the job itself doesn't change just because an employee likes it or doesn't like it. The job is simply still the job.

16

Luck has no place in autobiographies or motivational speeches.

Motivational speeches and inspiring autobiographies are supposed to tell us how we too can take control of our lives. "*See how Ms. Successful did it and how you can do it too*!" We buy into the stories and rhetoric just as we buy other things that help us take control and reshape our lives. Whether it is the food we wish to eat, a song we choose to hear on our stereos, or a speech we attend to pump us up, we only make purchases to take advantage of the purchase. Luck has no product or service that can be hocked. So why emphasize it?

17

Everything is 50/50.

Everything either did or did not. Everything either has or has not. Everything either is or is not. Regardless of how much we compile "evidence" and speculate, no one knows with any certainty whether anything will or will not. Therefore, regarding everything, there are two paths, equally possible. A chance of 50/50.

People who fail at many jobs often end up with the best jobs of all.

When employees continuously fail at jobs they've had there has obviously been mismatches of talent, capability, desire, and responsibility, between the positions and the employees who have filled them. That's okay. Sometimes it takes a while to find the right match. We expect this in the dating process: one failed relationship after another until individuals find their right matches. Sometimes it is early in life, sometimes later. By allowing an employee to explore so many possibilities, these "failed" individuals may be the luckiest workers of all, as they eventually find their particular niche where they can settle down, stop their running around, and gain complete job satisfaction.

Most people who don't worry about being fired always know they can sue.

One's "locus of control" determines whether people consider themselves responsible for their successes and failures or others responsible for their successes and failures. Employees, who tend to want to sue upon being fired, have an external locus of control, i.e. they believe their successes are theirs and their failures others'. Given this disposition, why wouldn't they sue for being fired? How could it be their fault? Perhaps it wasn't. Perhaps one was caught up in collateral damage. If the dismissal was unlawful, one should considering suing. Most dismissals, however, aren't unlawful. In fact, most employers will retain employees simply to avoid potential lawsuits. This allows those with an external locus of control not to worry.

Box Office Money

20

Whatever you would be willing to do for free is what you should be doing for a living. Everything else is for money.

Traditionally, when we leave the workplace, the world is a canvas we paint with our personal efforts and desires. We are usually not compensated financially for these efforts and do not expect to be. We give of ourselves freely, ultimately gaining satisfaction from being able to do so. Some people are lucky enough to spend their working days exactly the same way they would spend their personal lives. Those not living this way most likely have strong desires to be doing something else, something that leaves them more satisfied, more fulfilled, more worthwhile, more useful . . . happier. And with those strong desires, why else would they stay at their present jobs, other than for money?

21

What self-help books most inspire is the bank account of the author.

Inspiration is simply a "momentum" steroid. If the dosage isn't routinely and perpetually administered, the disease of lethargy eventually takes over. Momentum wanes, the patient becomes miserable, and, since few of us are capable of systematically delivering the dosage to ourselves, we return to the doctors who treat us with their injections of hopeful words. It's because our memories fade that those delivering the injections never run out of patients. The injections always cost us but the medicine comes cheap for those doctors of hope, and it comes in endless supply.

22

Luck doesn't sell well.

If a business pundit was to make a career from selling the notion that most of what happens is luck, he would go broke. People would quickly realize they don't need Chef Formula's recipe for business success were everything based on luck. That's why business solutions du jour, such as re-engineering and multi-national selling, barely address the power of luck. When Chef Formula finally is forced to address *luck*, he packages luck as something you can actually create. This fuels his lecture circuit and even more book signings. If he were to reveal the true power of luck people would realize they could just as well have that on their own.

23

When you wait for your raise, what you are really saying is, "Take control of my finances!"

However one rationalizes his or her patience for getting a raise, the patience exhibited is by choice. Mr. Passive's choice, whether it later appears to have been a good one or bad one, was a choice made in the context of Mr. Passive's financial profile. While a raise might only be a small portion of his financial profile, it is still a factor in it. Any power one gives to others in determining when and if a raise will occur is financial power one cedes. It's an easy concept to grasp when Mr. Passive buys stock in a company. Ironically, it is the same thing when an employee relinquishes control of his income to others, namely bosses who promise to do right by the employee, eventually.

SALES: Special Alliances Letting Everyone Spend

Sales won't take place without the establishment of relationships. Relationships, no matter how formal or informal, personal or impersonal, are at the heart of every business transaction involving the purchase of a good or service. Whether through a website, checkout counter, or $50 million dollar contract negotiation, a relationship marks the sales process. When many sales are made, many relationships are used. A salesperson's main objective is to create alliances with as many individuals or groups as possible. By doing so he hopes to enhance those relationships enough to let each alliance spend on his product or service.

25

There is more strength in money than in numbers.

The overriding aspect of business is to create income streams, else the business does not survive. Money is so powerful that it can even make profit more popular than what is already popular. Why else would cities sanction big fights when even the media denounces their worthiness? This distortion of popularity in a democratic society shepherds a point that eventually changes what is perceived as right. This is how lobbyists survive. While the voice of many may dictate what is popular, it does not, as a priority, dictate what is most profitable. The power of the masses, therefore, rarely takes priority of the power of money. Still when we see the examples, such as the government trading cigarette sales for increased taxes we are shocked.

26

Horrible products sold bring more money than superior products, which wait for their customers.

If you build it they will come? Not likely. They have to know about it to embrace it. And the only way they are going to know about it is through the marketing of it. Even word of mouth may suffice but without some sort of information distribution channel there is no way something will sell, no matter how good it is. And if it doesn't sell it will reap no reward regardless of how well it was constructed. Conversely, a poorly created product marketed well can reap millions. Just look at any item you buy from a dollar store. One dollar, one use, one break, one trash item.

27

Warrantees: papers that warrant teasing you they are worth more than the paper itself.

Warrantees, while touted as panaceas, mostly fall short of consumers' expectations. Most are neither read nor understood before the purchase that accompanies them. It's no wonder, with all of the legalese they contain. Warrantees, offered by Mr. Hardsell always seem to have some clause that makes you believe you are safe under all circumstances. Mr. Hardsell is all too happy to tease you into believing you are covered. Of course we all learn eventually, as soon as we call customer service and determine that our specific problem is the one problem not covered by the warrantee.

28

People who chase money find it more often than those who don't.

The average individual looks at the intense pursuit of money as greed that should be sublimated for more virtuous and laudable pursuits, such as job satisfaction, happiness, morality, ethics, and contribution. While those other pursuits are noteworthy, none promises financial gain. Money is simply another factor by which we pursue overall job satisfaction, no more or less intrinsically important than the other factors mentioned. By prioritizing money and being focused on money, *Moneyhunters* are more likely to steer their careers toward those transitions that better position them to gain money, just as with any other priority pursuit. This speaks nothing to the ideology of happiness once Moneyhunters have money. This merely states that Moneyhunters will have it. Whether or not Moneyhunters are happy at that point is related to every other facet of their lives.

29

Marketing, the single greatest tool of business, convinces people they are seeing through windows while they are looking through microscopes.

The purpose of marketing is to increase the probability that a selected group of individuals embraces a concept or product. Even if marketers want you to reject the concept or product, marketing is necessary. To succeed, marketers construct ways to have the selected group believe that conclusions drawn about products or concepts are their own. Because we draw conclusions about things based on what we know or learn about them, marketers ensure we learn only what supports embracing the product or idea. Simultaneously, marketers avoid teaching us everything else.

30

Nobody works for himself, though many people sign their own paychecks.

Treasurers of corporations as well as many entrepreneurs sign their own paychecks, but none is without a boss. Every employee works for someone, someone who provides direction for how to do his or her work. Entrepreneurs' bosses may not show up on their organizational charts, but they should. Above "President" or "CEO" it should read, "CUSTOMER." Above all employees in any organization it should read, "CUSTOMER," whether that customer is the boss or a population that buys their goods and services.

Businesses are set up to make money. That they employ people to run them is a necessary evil.

Unless an entrepreneur has an Attila complex, it's fairly certain that he or she did not set up the business to employ people, but to provide a service and sustain a living, however modest or comfortable. As businesses mature into corporations, employee costs increase, something counterproductive to the main objective of business, which is to stay in business. It is therefore unlikely that corporations would employ people unless employing them generated greater profits. When there is an opportunity to trade people for increased profits, the risk of not doing so increases the probability that the corporation will go out of business.

32

If teachers were paid 3 times what they are today, the world of teaching would consist of a very different population.

Teaching is a brutal profession and any teacher is certainly to be lauded. Because of its restrictive pay scale, however, the teaching profession has lost an unfathomable amount of highly talented, motivated, and intelligent group of individuals. Those who chose other professions were just as passionate about teaching and just as altruistic yet could not overcome the financial burden of the teaching pay scale nor the financial attractiveness of their talents and passions channeled in another more lucrative venture. If the teaching profession were to pay more it would breed a greater amount of competition for the distributed wealth. More would rush toward the money and through simple economics the overall value offered for the price would increase. The cream from a larger and more capable population would most likely supply the increased value.

33

Come up with a product you can mass market to fourteen-year-olds, and you will be a millionaire overnight.

Fourteen-year-olds, (FYTOs) probably have the greatest purchasing power of any population in our society. Old enough to know what they want without understanding all of the sacrifices involved, FYTOs are mostly devoid of social responsibilities associated with making a living. Still, these individuals are at an age where they too can work and make their "own" money through various means. FYTOs mostly acquire disposable income. They still get their meals and their clothes but that's someone else's concern. FYTOs' money is reserved for music, audio equipment, fad clothes, computer games, and other peripheral devices associated with their hobbies. If you produce what FYTOs want, they will acquire it, either by tapping into their parents' disposable income or by using their own disposable income with no fear of financial reprisal.

34

Horrible investments are most prevalent, yet they rarely make it into conversation.

Ignorance of market trends, poor financial advice, and timing cause many investors to lose money in their investments. To most investors, these seem like failures, bad decisions, a slight, or perhaps even a conspiracy to defraud them. These shortcomings aren't popularized because Mr. Bear doesn't want them reflecting upon him in any way. A fool and his money... Conversely, Mr. Bull, who excels in his investments, has no problem sharing his fortunate circumstances with others. That's because they reflect positively on him and paint a nicer picture, a picture he is much happier to have people see.

Jobs are simply relationships you get paid for.

Human contact in any job is inevitable. Just as people trade favors in their personal lives, employees trade their time for each other to ensure each succeeds at their respective position. The constant interaction of people to accomplish tasks supports the theory that we rely on each other to get jobs done, even if we believe we don't need them. Of course some employees interact better than others do. People who succeed at jobs succeed because they've found ways to thrive in their interaction with others. Even those whose human contact is consistently adversarial can remain if they relate well enough. Fortunately, most who do not interact well eventually find themselves dismissed before too long.

36

Price is the only thing that matters. Too often, we make money matter too.

We are conditioned to see a price in terms of the dollars we must spend to acquire a good or service. Retail stores posts their tags and business contracts have their bottom-line. How often do you see a tag that reads, "Will break in 2 years" or "Three of your weight-lifting buddies will have to help you carry this into your living room"? When you buy a service from someone, they don't write on the contract, "Your stress level will be reduced by 'X' amount" or "You will be demoted because of the time it takes to use our service." Instead, we get messages like 20% off and $599.99 and we focus on dollars, something that will be gone shortly. When all of the other considerations of price begin to emerge, too often it's too late.

37

$100,000 is not a lot of money.

Anyone who has made $100,000 in a calendar year knows it can be spent as quickly as any figure below it. With so many goods and services in our society begging to relieve us of our hard-earned money, no wonder people who make this level of income still struggle just as much as those who earn a lot less. True wealth does not come from making the heralded six-figure income but from making prudent and conservative decisions with any income one makes. Further, anyone who makes $100,000 knows he or she wants to make even more.

We are paid for our ability to perform repetitively not for what we think.

When customers purchase services from us, either as direct employees or service providers, we come with the expectation that we will repeat a past performance and produce a desired result. Our past experiences, gained from performing a certain way, show how we might reproduce those performances again and deliver predictable results. Selling well for companies A, B, and C, means we'll sell well for company D. Actions and not thoughts are how we promote our worthiness. While we may believe it's our brains that show our worth it is really our body's repeated behavior that convinces others of expected future results. If our bodies could not demonstrate repeatable and predictable behavior, it is unlikely that any company would invest in us to do anything for it.

Justice is always for sale.

Rarely do two people who violate rules end up with the same punishment. Too many factors determine an individual's ultimate punishment. Social reputation, promised future value, perceived character, and rationalization of the violation are but a few. The individual with greater financial backing can shine these factors, along with others, more favorably. A team of proponents for the violator can go to extraordinary lengths to shape one's reputation by performing exhaustive interviews until only the good ones are kept. The team can speak eloquently while framing many scenarios where society is harmed by punishing the individual. Finally, when necessary these same proponents can explain eloquently why, often with empirical data, the violator had no choice but to violate the rules put before him, truly believing the perpetrator acted the best way possible given the particular situation. And the entire defense starts with money.

40

Teams need only promise to be good; there will always be supporters willing to pay top dollar for hope no matter how fleeting.

Promising mediocrity would be suicidal for any team attempting to garner the support of sponsors or patrons. Teams, athletic or corporate, garner support by selling the hope of great success: success the sponsors and patrons will want to share. If they didn't sell hope teams would never get the backing they desire. Teams promote what is possible in an effort to convince supporters that this is the time when the team will finally come through. Sponsors and patrons then support them financially, either by funding their efforts or participating in their performance. Hope for the team's success compels others to buy into the notion that this time they will be victorious. The cycle repeats itself because the law of averages supports a notion that the team must succeed eventually, regardless of what past performance indicates.

41

Great compensation is reserved for those who either produce great revenue or reduce great expense.

Businesses produce revenue and incur expenses. And those who make the company money make money. This is why salespeople generally out-earn all other employees in a corporation. This is also why high-level executives, charged with efficiently managing the expenses of their organization, are given huge stock options and inflated salaries. When an employee believes she greatly influences high revenues or reduced expenses and can demonstrate that, she has a pretty solid case for increased compensation in whatever forms are available through the organization. Unfortunately, most of us deem our value from hard work, a good attitude, and a team orientation. Laudable but rarely financially translatable.

PROFIT:
Professionals Redirecting Others Finances Into Theirs

To profit in any endeavor, companies must find ways to produce more revenue than expenses. This happens either by reducing expenses or by increasing revenue. Either way, the revenue has to come from somewhere. If the company's only revenue comes from inside the company, this accounting trick will eventually submerge the business. Therefore, if companies want profit they must find ways to amass revenue from sources other than their own pockets, i.e. the finances of others. The more a company can direct others' finances toward the company the more profitable that company can be.

43

The odds are the richest kid to graduate from a high school class won't be the class valedictorian.

The misconception we are taught in our youth, probably so that we will study, is that succeeding at school means succeeding in life. Because we so often measure success in financial terms, we extrapolate the success-at-school axiom into the notion that great grades translate into great money. Financial success, however, involves great decision-making, moderate risk, luck, tenacity, timing, and the building of good relationships, none of which is the cornerstone of academic achievement. Conversely, great grades mostly can be achieved in a vacuum. Becoming the class valedictorian might ensure an ivy education and an above-average income, but it certainly will not guarantee or even suggest financial wealth.

44

Salaries are a function of perceived value; education, experience, and expertise, no matter how great, often pale in comparison to that perception.

Despite all of the salary surveys available salaries are not an exact science. Salaries are paid because someone with salary-compensating power perceives that the employee deserves it. It doesn't really matter whether or not everyone else, the employee included, believes the employee is being compensated "fairly." The problem others have with employees' salaries is that their perceived value of these employees differs from the authority figure determining the employees' salaries. Employment laws and corporate policies hope to negate this disparity. But too many intangibles exist such as negotiation skills and perception of one's ability that demonstrates why one employee makes more than another when it appears they should be compensated equally.

Everyone works hard...just ask them.

Who would admit to being a lazy sack of garbage at his job? Who would promote herself as a non-contributor? We work with all sorts of people performing at all sorts of levels. Some are highly contributory; some certainly aren't. But those that aren't don't see it that way. They see themselves just as integral as the ones who carry the corporate load. Some know they don't contribute but pretend they make the corporation run like a well-oiled machine. If you interview all employees, they'll consistently promote their own worthiness. Don't be surprised when those you deem worthless shower you with their self-congratulatory insight.

46

People who work really really hard are often viewed as underachievers.

When you work really hard, people certainly will appreciate your efforts. But will they perceive what you desire? When others notice your excessive work efforts, they'll likely question why you work so hard. Is it your dedication, commitment, love of work? Or is it simply that you can't do your job as well as the others in positions like yours? Maybe it's something as simple as having no life outside the office. Who cares what the real reason is? That people would even consider you inept or socially unbalanced is enough to keep you grounded in your position much longer than you desire.

47

Sometimes people just lose, and it doesn't matter how hard they tried.

We get too caught up in the belief that we can control outcomes simply by putting out more sweat from ourselves than our opponents do. Whether it's a job-hunting exercise, sporting event, or the closing of a sale, we believe there is a direct correlation between how hard we try and what we should get as a result of trying so hard. But how hard we try often cannot overcome another's superior talent, our own bad luck or timing, or, in the case of job hunting and sales, a superior recommendation afforded to one of our competitors.

There is someone who will learn in 3 years what took you 10.

If there is anything you have learned faster than someone else, you have to believe there is someone out there who has learned that same thing faster than you. Skills track the same way. While time moves at the same speed for everyone, individuals use time very differently. Consider one's knowledge and experience as a set of questions on a test that need to be answered for one to develop an understanding of something. No matter how quickly you can read the questions and write your answers someone else can do either of those tasks or even both of those tasks faster than you and still get a better score than you. In other words, they presumably went through everything you did but faster and more proficient. Isn't this what you have done to learn things faster than other people have?

Most incompetent people are not fired.

Firing poor performers is a very difficult proposition, both legally and logistically. It often involves large amounts of documentation as well as personal and objective reviews. Most bosses would rather just concentrate on work and live with the hope that incompetent employees will eventually improve. With all the interviews, phone calls, and the angst in trying to replace an ineffective employee, no wonder managers and supervisors let themselves suffer with ineffective talent far longer than they should. Besides, nobody is completely ineffective 100% of the time. So managers rationalize through these glimmers of hope that ineffective employees are still worth keeping. Besides, complaining about them to other employees is so much more fun!

50

If no one "dropped the ball," companies would be a lot smaller.

Companies grow because more people are brought in to solve a company's problems that the present staff cannot seem to solve. This happens when employees either make mistakes or do not possess requisite skills. No employee is omniscient when embarking on a task. This creates an opportunity for inefficiency. When groups attack a task, the opportunity for inefficiency increases. Alas, companies are comprised of individuals and those individuals are fallible. If employees or groups solved problems better than they currently do or had greater skills than they currently have, companies would run more efficiently. With this greater efficiency, staffing requirements would lessen. This is why companies reduce staff when forced to operate more efficiently.

If you are the best person for the job, sometimes you are even lucky enough to get that job.

The best person for the job is the one who will: 1) best perform the job, 2) best represent the position of the job within and outside of the company, and 3) add something that will enhance the job for the next person who assumes it. That said, is the best person for a job always the incumbent? Probably not. The incumbent is the one who got the job by a variety of means, such as interviewing for the job or being lucky enough to be handed the job. Other ways of securing a position include: 1) the only other course of action was a termination, 2) nepotism, 3) no one else was available for hire at the time, 4) the position isn't important enough to go to extensive lengths to hire the best person for it, and 5) the best person didn't launch a successful enough campaign to get noticed. While the incumbent might really be the best person for the job, it is more likely the incumbent was best situated to get the job and not necessarily the best person for the job.

DEGREE:
Document Endorsing Great Rewards Erroneously Espoused

See COLLEGE!

Brains do not equate to money, nor does talent. Neither grades nor degrees equate to success. All are nice to have though, as they make great conversation.

Sterling credentials always present well. Anyone who has a problem with them has no appreciation of the efforts and sacrifices one went through to obtain them. Whether it is brains, talent, grades, or degrees, all promote well, even it is only for self-promotion. However, the lessons of life teach us that these credentials are merely tools that one must exploit (along with many other things like risk, good decision-making, and relationships) to be successful. Moreover, there is no guarantee that any credential alone will reap financial or any other success. It is merely how one applies that credential that enhances the probability of success, an application many of us never learn to make.

Everyone always gives 100%. We just change the percentage-scale to fit the result.

We witness Mr. Performer produce certain results then expect him to repeat those results each successive time Mr. Performer performs. This is the fallacy of perfect effort. Circumstances, i.e., inside and outside influences, always change, no matter how they appear not to have. Our lack of appreciation of how the current circumstances affected Mr. Performer is what makes us espouse his less-than-perfect effort. Our expectations for what we feel he should have accomplished aren't met, and we immediately blame Mr. Performer for not trying hard enough, i.e., not giving 100 percent. We rarely notice the changes in his influences because we are too focused on our own expected results for him.

55

Showing humility is one of the best ways to say, "I am the best." Saying "I am the best!" is another great way.

Being humble raises others' opinions of you to the point where you are actually considered superior. So few people are truly humble and by expressing humility, your slot in the food chain elevates. Dually, stating out loud with professed arrogance and self-assuredness that you are "the best" makes others actually consider your assertion of superiority. Others may disagree with you, wishing desperately to knock you from your high horse. But in their desire to challenge you, they have lent credibility to your proclamation. Further, those who do not challenge you are content to let you live the proclamation and all of the glory that comes with it (even if they may also think you're a pompous jerk.)

56

People who are really good at something are probably even better at something else.

People are not one-dimensional, no matter how much others try to slot them by the jobs they perform. Our society labels people, usually by something we've witnessed about them. The better they perform, the deeper we brand them. Sometimes the brand gets so deep that the thought of them excelling at something completely different seems ludicrous. After all, how could Ms. Salescloser also be the best computer analyst? That we don't conceive of her having multiple abilities is even more ludicrous than singularly branding her. There are countless examples of duo-stars, but the promotion of these double-hitters is scant. Otherwise, we'd be stuck spending more time understanding each other and embracing the countless possibilities each of us offers. Labeling each other is so much easier.

57

Just because you are paid to do something does not make you an expert in that something.

Presumably most of us are paid for the jobs we perform. And it is reasonable to expect that an individual will develop a modicum of skill in a job just by performing in that job. But there is a significant difference between an expert and a performer. A performer can endure the responsibilities of a position and continue to maintain the position. An expert is superior in a given task or position, is better than most, and understands all nuances of the task or position, not just how to execute it proficiently. Nowhere in the definition of expert does it suggest that if you are compensated for a task or position you are afforded the label of expert. Further, many people are experts at things for which they are never compensated financially.

Everyone has problems: winners just know how to unload them onto others quickly.

If you're alive, you have problems and they don't cease until you stop living. Our ability to solve them is one of our greatest assets. People who can solve problems are justifiably thought of as winners and many of them are compensated greatly for their problem-solving prowess. Business is essentially the provision of a solution to a problem. And in business, perhaps the fastest way to solve a problem is to pass it along. Of course, this is done with adroit slight-of-hand. "*That sounds like a problem for Mr. Solution*," or "*The department you really need to deal with is The Land of We Want All Problems*," also known as customer support. Once successfully passed, the winner is freed of his own problem-solving responsibilities, while simultaneously being able to promote himself as a problem-solver.

59

90% effort is good enough 99% of the time.

If you've ever tried really hard to solve a business problem, you've probably rationalized that you gave about a 90% effort. If you've ever tried really, really, really hard, so much that you thought you would pop a blood vessel in your head, you probably rationalized that you gave 100%. Few of us solve all problems with veins popping out of our heads. If we did, we'd go insane. Yet even with our reduced level of problem-solving effort, things somehow have worked out anyway. This is because it takes almost as much time and effort to go from 90% to 100% as it does to go from 0% to 90%. We tolerate ours as well as others' levels of 90% because time is so important in business transactions. And the quicker we accept one's effort toward solving a problem, the more quickly we can deploy that person to their next effort.

Promotions are businesses' way of telling you you're cheaper to keep than to dismiss.

If businesses didn't need your services, they would surely dismiss you. As nice as you may be to look at, you exist because your employer thinks you have value. Promoting you is a way that holds on to you and avoids the expense of letting you go. Perhaps if you were fired, you'd take with you knowledge, clients, or even the entire marketing unit. Those are risks the company is unwilling to take. What better way to play on your notion of loyalty than to extend the regal carrot of a glorified title?

When someone says, "I've given my best," what they are really saying is, "I refuse to do anymore and if you want me to, go to hell."

The presumption of giving one's best is that you have exhausted every effort possible to perform any more than what you could. Perhaps Mrs. Nomoreleft didn't get the result she wanted from her effort, but alas, she gave it her all. Having to justify her effort to a boss or anyone else by openly stating, "I did my best," immediately puts Mrs. Nomoreleft in a defensive position she most likely doesn't appreciate. She really can say nothing more in her defense after she's made her claim because by giving her best she has done everything she could; everything else would just be an excuse. So she remains righteous by her claim, and if her boss is still dissatisfied he can simply take a direct path to the underworld.

RESUME: Rambling Exaggerations So Unsuspecting Management Employs.

Has anyone ever put together a resume without an exaggeration or twelve? Resumes in their purest form are advertisements promoting an individual. Just like the ads we see on television and in the newspaper, they purport a foundation of truth wrapped by an attractive representation of it. The advertisement is designed to coax an unaware organization into 1) believing that the attractive representation of the truth is just as true as the foundation it surrounds and 2) seeking the employment of the advertised individual.

63

Too often we explain effect with cause, when in fact, effect is simply effect.

We seek so much to understand the why, how, and what, of circumstances that have taken place to ensure they will or will not happen again. In other words, we try to control outcomes through replication. Subsequently, we teach ourselves which actions will ensure which outcomes. Nothing is repeatable, however, because no time, space, and circumstance collaborations are equally pliable. Time continues, space changes, and circumstances, no matter how similar, are not exact. Therefore, no expected "effect" can ever be perfectly explained with a specific "cause." This is why better teams lose to inferior teams and why some people make more money than others, when their jobs seem to be equal. *Effect* is simply "Effect" because that outcome is the only thing true about the circumstances that occurred.

People who are better than you in some things are probably better than you at most things.

Our sense of fair play has us believing in a give-and-take society: that is, if you are Ms. Talented at one thing, then something else must be sacrificed for you to be good at that one thing. This is a fallacy cloaked by the fact that superiorly skilled individuals don't have unlimited amounts of time. Being good at one thing merely relates to 1) experience with that thing and 2) natural ability with that thing. The base skills a person uses to do things, such as running, artistry, relationship building, and logical problem solving, are portable to most of the other things Ms. Talented can do. But she doesn't have forever to do everything. And while you might be better than Ms. Talented at something initially, if she has superior base skills to perform the task you are performing, in time she will outperform you.

Expert users are nothing more than androids.

Teams develop software packages, perhaps a team consisting of only one member. When the package was created that team decided; what the software would do and how, when the software would be able to do what it does, and under which circumstances the software would work. Essentially, the team created the software to control all users actions a priori. Most users just do not realize this, especially with complicated and sophisticated software packages. Being an extremely proficient user merely demonstrates a superior ability at following instructions, something a sophisticated robot might do.

Your personality follows you from job to job. All facets of one job will eventually show itself in the next.

People don't change just because they change jobs. While they learn new things and learn new ways of solving old problems the base elements of one's personality: drive, organizational skills, brainpower, and passion for work, move with the employee from position to position. Thriving in one position and failing in another is more than likely due to the system one operates in and how she is utilized more than her having skill in one job and all of a sudden losing it in the next. Over time she will infuse every aspect of her personality from her last job into the current one. People who consistently succeed at jobs are either: 1) very versatile or 2) not very versatile and lucky to continue in similar systems.

Discrimination is keeping your least effective employee.

Finding one corporation where one of its policies is to keep its least effective employee on the corporate payroll would be nearly impossible. If corporations allowed their least effective employees to stay on the corporate payroll, they would likely be acting on prejudice, an unfavorable or favorable feeling formed without knowledge. With knowledge of an employee's ineffectiveness keeping that employee wouldn't make business sense. Therefore, in order for the employee to remain, there is either no knowledge of the employee's ineffectiveness or there is knowledge combined with some other form of prejudice. That prejudice comes either in unfavorable forms such as favoritism, racism, or nepotism, or favorable forms such as hope and compassion. Whether favorable or unfavorable, prejudice still is the compelling notion to retain the ineffective employee. And acting upon prejudice is discrimination.

The more an employee apologizes, the less they are sorry.

As in relationships, people eventually grow tired of the same rhetoric offered from situation to situation. When an employee constantly apologizes for mistakes he has made, the verity of that apology loses its luster. Soon when Mr. Regretful apologizes, he is more likely to be met with an abrupt, "I KNOW" rather than a consoling, "Don't worry about it." At this point, neither Mr. Regretful nor the one who regrets his misgiving is satisfied. Mr. Regretful's apology comes almost by routine rather than by admission of guilt. Further, when the habit of apologizing marks Mr. Regretful, he solidifies the impression that he may screw up anything so long as he apologizes. This further undermines the credibility of his apology and leaves others wondering whether he even knows why he is apologizing.

69

The harder you work, the more self-congratulatory you become.

We all want to feel good about the great effort we expend in any endeavor. Why not? Expending great effort is taxing, grueling, and often leaves us beaten. Without being able to feel good about the effort, we'd have little incentive to repeat it. So often, because that good feeling is all we have to take from the effort, we are justified in feeling good about it. And the greater the effort, the better the feeling. Sure it'd be nice to get a pat on the back but most of our great efforts go unnoticed. When others are around, however, we have a greater tendency to share our renewed sense of self with them, i.e., brag. Even the most humble of us have someone who will endure the puffing of our chests. And we are all too glad to share our fortune with them.

70

Whether you are part of the solution or part of the problem depends more on reputation than on circumstances.

Nearly every corporate department has a Starchild; the employee who most believe can solve any problem put before him. Dually, there is the counterpart employee, the one believed incapable of solving the number of degrees in a right angle: Crossedchild. With all the problems that arise in a business department, the odds are insurmountably against the notion that Starchild can always solve the problem better than Crossedchild. Further, when Starchild cannot solve the problem the problem is deemed unsolvable, that is, until Crossedchild solves it, of course while no one is looking. Starchild gets an excuse for not solving the problem and the next time a problem arises, Starchild is consulted again.

Most people think saying "it" actually means "it!"

If saying "it" actually meant "it," the phrase, "Show me, don't tell me" wouldn't have so much validity in negotiations. Politicians and corporate leaders know this better than most. That is why their words are so carefully chosen, right down to the adjectives and verbs. So often their words inspire us that we lose sight of the fact that no actions have actually taken place. Alas, the point of action arises and the words no longer carry their previous merit. When one acts without words, an indisputable message is sent. When one speaks instead of acts, the message becomes one of debate, which immediately casts doubt on the validity of the statement.

72

Creative people need not label themselves such.

While anyone can profess a creative nature, no one should pay much attention to the assertion. It's almost as banal as proclaiming that you breathe. Everyone is creative. Everyone. Creativity has so many manifestations that nearly everyone breathing can exhibit some form of it. They might exhibit it in something simple like loading the dishwasher or in something complex like making new computer software. We believe certain jobs to be more creative than others, but this is simply the lack of recognition of other forms of creativity. Further, anyone looking for imagination from another will find it. It needn't be worn like a badge of honor. If the creativity is truly exhibited, it will precede the individual.

73

Responsibility is overrated and underappreciated.

Too often, we correlate increased responsibility with greater importance and effectiveness rationalizing that assuming more responsibility will lead to financial reward and a grander lifestyle. But increased responsibility more often leads to increased stress and headaches, two things that cut into that grander lifestyle we envision for ourselves. We might say that increased responsibility is justified because it helps us evolve. While some financial reward may ease our growth, consider that consultants are compensated high above most employees, have the least amount of accountability, are listened to the most by executive management, and rarely worry about being appreciated at all.

74

In life we call it conniving, shrewd, deceitful, and manipulative; in business we call it strategic.

All's fair in love and war should really read, "All's fair in business." Characteristics we would absolutely abhor about an individual, we tend to put up with in business, especially when they yield the business results we want. If your boyfriend or girlfriend gave you an ultimatum, you would probably ditch him or her. If your spouse shrewdly negotiated with you for every transaction that took place between you, he or she might drive you insane. Nevertheless, business dealings lose this veil of scrutiny and gain the latitude of permissibility because we don't assign morality, honesty, and integrity to business. Of course we want those things in our business dealings, we just don't think of them as the primary foundation for a business transaction. We are simply too concerned with the finished transaction and our own responsibility to ensure that we got a good deal.

75

No matter how positive your attitude, 99% of all problems need action and not attitude to be solved.

No one can fault a person for having a great attitude, even in the direst of circumstances. Having a great attitude opens yourself to possibilities you might not have seen if you stewed in frustration over a given set of circumstances. But because attitude occurs in the mind, it only solves problems of the mind. Other than brain disease, and maybe a few psychosomatic illnesses, every problem we face occurs outside of our mind, and to deal with that problem we must take action. At most, action might be vehemently working to change the world-At least, action might be working to change our current attitude.

Thou shalt.

Break the law? I don't think so. However, there are about a billion actions we can take that are ethical, moral, and legal that we never do. Yet we come up with an equal billion reasons why we shouldn't act. And every single one of those inactions is rooted in some form of fear. Ironically fear is the greatest motivator to act, and equally the greatest motivator not to act. We act when we confront the fear and not when we eschew it.

77

Each trait an employee possesses always has two names: one used by the people who admire and/or respect them, and one used by the people who fear and/or loathe them.

Whether we like employees or not has no bearing on what those employees are, only how we tend to perceive them. When we deal with Ms. Likeable we try to see good in her, inspecting quality into her, just as line managers might inspect quality into a product. When she doesn't pass inspection, we just fib on her paperwork. But when we deal with Mr. Disdain, we tend to do just the opposite, discrediting him instead of taking him at face value. We view Ms. Likeable as tenacious, Mr. Disdain as aggressive. Ms. Likeable is confident; Mr. Disdain is arrogant. Ms. Likeable is brilliant; Mr. Disdain is a know-it-all.

78

Self-righteousness is its own reward. Pity it rarely translates into money, a promotion, another's respect, or peace of mind.

We are taught to avoid bad-tempered and judgmental behavior, to work hard, to be on time, and to avoid sycophancy. We then pat ourselves on the back for being good corporate soldiers. Too often, however, we watch others get ahead through means we've been taught to disdain. Sure, we point out the inconsistencies, but rarely do things change for us because of our assertions. Instead, we are left to laud ourselves publicly or privately because we did not behave as they did. At the end of the day, they have the promotion, the increased salary, the increased exposure, and the corner office. We however, have our pride and absolutely no desire to poison their coffee.

79

"Don't get caught up in the details," means "I don't care what the details are."

Choosing whether or not to focus on details is not entirely condemnable. The argument will always exist as to which is better, hardnosed detail orientation or sexy big-picture focus. Unfortunately both are necessary, but many see their role as only being concerned with the bigger picture. Being forced to concentrate on details when an employee doesn't want to presents an immediate conflict. Self-appointed "Big Pix" view the crossing of T's and the dotting of I's as a "*straightening of the desk*," which more often leads to inertia than progress. Big Pix argue that nothing is served by ensuring that processes are completely followed when the processes themselves are flawed. It doesn't matter whether "Big Pix" are right or wrong. Time will certainly prove whether they were or not.

80

Grandmothers can't be taught to do a lot, despite how easily you think you could teach them.

It is very popular to inform young Mr. Inept, who is struggling with a new concept or task that "your grandmother" could perform better than he. "Grandma could wire that circuit." "Grandma could load that software program." Not likely. It is far more probable that grandmothers, who 1) make up a considerable part of the aged society, 2) are admittedly not as active, and 3) are probably not in as good health, are unwilling to learn new methodologies. Both their reluctance to learning and their physical challenges are not altogether compatible with their ease of skill enhancement.

81

When you wait for your promotion, what you are really saying is, "Take control of my future!"

Exercising your patience is whose choice? It's yours, of course. Whatever your reason for waiting, you chose to wait. If a promotion was promised, perhaps it will even come. But the patience and trust you've put in others to ensure your "just" reward was a leap of faith, nothing more. Circumstances could change just before you're promoted that prohibit you from ever being promoted. The company could file bankruptcy, your boss could quit, or a promotion freeze could hit. Why wait? If you do, you are putting your fate in the hands of the organization. If you are truly promotable, shouldn't you be a little more proactive? It's a quality you most likely exhibited to be considered for a promotion in the first place.

82

The underachiever asks, "Why?" The visionary asks, "Why not? The genius asks, "Why bother?"

Underachievers typically see the mountain long before they see the valley that lies just beyond it or just in front of it. Their lack of appreciation for what is possible causes them to see roadblocks in business instead of the benefits of realizing corporate goals. Visionaries, ever steadfast in the possibilities they can see, see relatively few if any obstacles, and therefore say "Why not?" to just about everything. The genius, however, sees the futility of every effort, and that ultimately, we are born and we die, and everything in between is simply a game we play to amuse ourselves. Geniuses understand that the game creates a great deal many mock winners: those who have struggled for "greatness," only to meet their maker, just as everyone eventually will.

83

Great heart makes for wonderful stories, but skill is better. Most losers wanted it a lot more than the winners that beat them.

Had David and Goliath gone ten rounds, it is a sure bet that David would have ended up a pancake. Beating Goliath is the dream we sell to underdogs all across the lands. "Take that one shot and you have a chance no matter how small that chance appears." The marketing of this idea has inspired untold millions in one form or another. But the reality of it is that people with natural superior talent and skill usually win out over those who try hard. Sure, talent and skill can be developed within the inferiorly talented individual. However, those with greater natural skill start out ten steps ahead of the game. And if those people choose to develop that talent, the one with inferior talent has a David's chance of beating them, no matter how badly they may want to win.

Lasting impressions are the most accurate.

Lasting impressions build up over time. While first impressions may never change, more often than not employees have chances to make not only one but several impressions. During their tenure employees will either reinforce or change their impressions through their repeated efforts. Once gone, these impressions, good or bad, tend to grow proportionately over time like yarns of tales long ago. This happens in the short term because employees' impressions are more the product of other's emotions towards them at the time of their departure. In the long term, however, these impressions subside as more and more about the employee is remembered. Eventually the settled impression is the one that others should have had all along.

People who lack creativity love to label things "useless."

It is very easy to label something useless or unimportant, such as ninth-grade algebra. Being creative often requires great effort and a desire to see past the "useless" axiom. Still, most of us believe creativity just happens naturally. Lacking creativity is more about laziness than natural talent. Only by opening our minds to the possibilities that lie within every piece of knowledge or every instrument do we gain true appreciation for something's existence.

Everyone judges everyone all the time; only sometimes do our judgments affect our behavior.

People who don't judge don't think. It's impossible to see something and not draw a conclusion about it. It all goes back to the conundrum, "If you choose not to decide, you still have made a choice." Not judging is a judgment. Neutralites like to claim they are not judgmental and even appear to be when their judgment does not bring judgment upon them. But Neutralites are still judging, it's just that their judgment hasn't motivated them to action or combative speech. Eventually, when something else comes along and pushes their activity buttons, you can bet Neutralites will rationalize that their judgment is justified.

87

Practicing is not popular, many times not necessary, but always virtuous.

If a survey was taken within any group whose mission was to put on an eventual performance, say a play, a sporting event, or a presentation before a board meeting, there is a strong chance most of those surveyed would rather not have to practice. Practicing is always for something else other than practice itself, and that distinction gives practice its noble quality. But is practice really necessary? It is for some, but not for all. Practicing is intended to elevate one's capabilities to perform at a certain level to gain an acceptable achievement. And practicing mostly does this. However, many groups, and individuals as well, can gain that acceptable achievement level simply by using their natural talents, being lucky, or manipulating circumstances so that their lack of practice is not evident. Only when the acceptable level of achievement is not reached do we question whether or not the individual or group practiced enough.

Most people realize that the number of people who really care what they do for a living wouldn't fill a stadium. Yet they strike out at athletes anyway.

The ritual of watching sports allows us to release our emotions, emotions we rarely have the luxury of sharing elsewhere. These come out even more when we see athletes gaining preferential treatment and large incomes. We wonder why those who have athletic "gifts" reap so much, when most of the general public does not. This is simply Economics 101 and we are responsible. We consciously choose to financially empower athletes, either by attending their performances, watching them on television, or purchasing trinkets associated with them. Conversely, what most of us do for a living would neither remotely excite the general public nor inspire them to actively invest in us.

PRODUCTION SCHEDULE
JIM
BOB
SUE
KIM
LEX
Jim
Just say "No"

The more you say "no," the more others will do for you.

There is a phenomenon that occurs at all levels in the corporation called the NMJ syndrome: "not my job". This mindset excuses task assignees who deem themselves too important from performing certain tasks. Alas, the task still needs to be done, but Mr. NMJ has refused. Instead of whacking him on the head, you and/or others take on the task, ensuring a more stable work environment. Consequently, Mr. NMJ has made you respect his time more than your own.

90

If the impetus is there, corporate decisions can be made with little or no discussion.

It's ironic that companies can immediately change an employee's salary once an employee has made it clear he will no longer work for the wage he currently makes. Companies use leverage, whereby the company borrows money from you for as long as possible before it has to pay you what you are really worth. Company leaders hedge by asking for detailed analysis and justification for new salaries or other expense then attempt to wait until the next occurrence of Halley's comet to act. This is because pushing company expenses out by even one day can translate into huge savings for the company. But when decisions HAVE to be made, meetings are not necessary, corporate vice-presidents don't have to take three weeks, and boards of directors don't have to be consulted. This is why employees find out their real worth only when they announce their intended departure.

Synergy markets very well. Were it not for people, merging companies might actually achieve it.

Companies partner with other companies so that 1+1=3 instead of 2. The promise of this equation to the public, investors, and requisite employees, causes stocks to rise and CEOs to get rich. But the efforts to realize the equation more often do harm than good to the overall corporate partnership. Newly created partnerships inevitably must endure the following: 1) political competition at all levels, 2) excessive spending to buy out displaced executives and other employees, 3) dried-up sales-distribution channels that were expected to thrive, and 4) more complex business transactions. Taking these factors into account, why synergize at all? Because if you can eat faster than another, chances are you'll end up with more of the pizza. But if you are the only eater, you can eat the whole pizza, no matter how slowly you eat.

92

Nothing is as easy as you think it is or as difficult as others would like you to believe.

The beauty of our creative minds is to see what's possible before it takes form: to dream. Havoc is wreaked when we see for ourselves what's possible without seeing the barriers in the way. We see ourselves as musclemen on the beach with beautiful girls, but we don't see the 4,000 hours of weight training. We see ourselves litigating high profile cases, but we don't see ourselves pouring through hundreds of law books. These obstacles are just as real as our dreams, but we lose sight of them. We save seeing obstacles for others' dreams (and proudly profess them when others share their dreams with us). Our view of others' obstacles is exaggerated by our envy at their attempt at greatness compounded with the fear that we should attempt what they're attempting.

93

The larger the company, the greater the chance someone works there who shouldn't.

People are hired for all sorts of reasons, and as companies grow employees come to the organization through increased channels. Hiring organizations are like border patrol with staffers gate-keeping company forces. As well as these gatekeepers work, the sheer volume of employees entering the organization through different means will eventually overwhelm them. Inevitably, "ineffectives" will slip past them when they had little or no business doing so. Although these "ineffectives" add nothing to the company's welfare, removing them is often difficult. The greater the organization, the more likely the number of "ineffectives" present.

94

Processes do not change until someone who influences the process becomes a victim of the process.

Too often governing bodies make policies and processes and never anticipate living by them. Do you think the director of customer service for a Fortune 500 company punches through twelve phone numbers and sits on hold for half an hour to get his problem solved? Not likely. Only when the restrictive nature of his process prohibits Mr. Policymaker does he realize just how flawed the process is. And if the victim of the process is his boss or someone with equal influence over the policymaking body, LOOK OUT! Until then, the ranting of those affected by the process merely falls on deaf ears.

Most decisions are made long before we are asked to make them. Our wait is merely a courtesy of our asker.

We know what we want, long before someone asks us. Either we don't have the guts to state it openly or the moment of truth, when we have to reveal our decisions openly, has not yet arrived. Until then it is very easy to avoid potential confrontations behind such veils as "I don't know" and "I need some time to weigh my options." The courtesy really is ours, afforded by those asking of us. We've been given the time and consideration to decide something. But we already knew what the decision was and now we must find a way to state it.

96

TEAMWORK:
Tempering Excellence Achieved Monopolistically While Onlookers Reap Kudos

Most people work in teams of one form or another. While we all like to believe that teams consist of equal contributors, in reality every team has a Most Valuable Contributor. Advocating that may be politically incorrect, but the MVC exists, regardless of whether or not that MVC is a jerk. In sports, this ideology is not only promoted but is expected. In business, however, it is quite unpopular. In the interest of fairness for all team members companies have attempted to subvert the promotion of an MVC, thus catering to and protecting employees' feelings. But MVC's cannot altogether be crushed. And through their existence other team manifestations arise including employees' sycophancy and the resentment and sabotage of other team members.

97

We call it business for no other reason than it is what keeps us most busy.

The root word "busy" linked with the suffix "ness" is really just a way of turning the word "busy" into a more prolific noun. However prolific, its origin is still what Webster calls "actively and attentively engaged." Meetings are the best opportunity to be attentively and actively engaged. Business, however, is about generating revenue and managing expenses, regardless of the activities employees muster for themselves. Unfortunately, employees spend too much time "actively and attentively engaged" and not enough time creating more money for the organization.

98

Marketing plans are nothing more than legal conspiracy.

Marketing plans, as elaborate as the national rollout of a new line of automobiles or as simple as marketing bottled water on the beach, are designed to make people or companies buy. Through the careful placement, positioning, pricing, and promotion of items, services, or ideas, purchases are coerced and too often we don't even realize it. Like the items at a grocery store checkout or the phone calls we receive only when we happen to be home, marketing minds have gone to great lengths to control our behavior. Sometimes the plans involve pictures, words, and activities. Sometimes the plans involve thousands of agents each playing their specific role. Regardless of the coercion vehicle used, all vehicles are directed toward the singular effort of driving purchasers to purchase.

Systems are set up by self-appointed experts to control behavior of those deemed sheep. By participating in the system, those deemed sheep have in fact christened themselves such.

Regarding Darwinian business evolution, rule-makers preen atop Mt. Everest and somewhere; perhaps a foot above the floor of the Marianna Trench are rule-followers. Rule-makers set up the systems of the corporation under the guise that they know what will make the company operate most efficiently. Most of the time, rule-makers act in small groups, rarely permitting the input or consent of rule-followers, those who will eventually put to task what the rule-makers deem appropriate. It's the rule-followers' compliance, either by rule-makers' coercion of them or their own lack of knowledge, which purports that rule-followers should be rule-followers and never evolve to the more prestigious position of rule-maker.

100

Details are for people without sales skills.

Salespeople create income streams, and the rest of the corporation manages expenses. These expenses come in many forms, such as administration, research, marketing, and technical support, but ultimately each of these departments is simply spending the money the salespeople brought into the firm. Further, salespeople only concern themselves with one detail: meeting quota. All other details of the corporation, such as budgets, spending, forecasting, and planning, are someone else's responsibilities.

Companies hire and fire employees because piling employees onto a problem rarely solves a problem faster.

Good leaders within organizations know that problem solving does not come from throwing money at problems but by coming up with smart and creative solutions. Money is the scapegoat poor leaders use as the excuse for not solving a problem. This is why budgets are scrutinized and excessive spending is frowned upon in any organization. Body-throwers create the same waste. Employees represent costs to an organization. When leaders haphazardly tie up employees without truly analyzing and understanding how the problem can best be solved, additional headcount won't matter. Too often Body-throwers learn this in hindsight, realizing "smarter is better" instead of "more is better." Unfortunately, the additional employees who represent these cost overruns must be released to mitigate staffing expenses that never should have taken place.

102

Customer-Deflection Departments: a zillion under-appreciated middle-class Americans paid dirt wages, who pretend to care about customers' problems.

How can you pay someone to care? Money doesn't make people care, caring does! Anyone who has called a customer-service department knows the frustration so many companies create for customer-service inquirers. Customer deflectors too often try to finish calls prematurely, long before the real issue is solved. They disconnect you, or better, put you on hold forever. Why not? They don't make a great deal of money, are rarely if ever appreciated, and are often spoken to like they're idiots. Moving callers to another agent or even better, another department, lets them deflect their problem (you) in another direction. It's nearly impossible to get "your" deflector twice, let alone twice in a row, and for good reason. Once deflected, you are supposed to stay deflected. It's the one true sanctity a deflector has.

The best charities are run like the best corporations.

Charities, in order to survive must manage their expenses and generate continuous streams of revenue. This is done through constant campaigning for money (sales) and through shrewd back-office management (finance.) Charities must creatively invent new ways to garner money from consumers and corporations (R&D) and provide literature and justification to the public as to why the charity deserves the public's dollars (marketing.) Tax considerations included, charities die off without performing profitably in each of the above corporate-related areas.

104

Teams are necessary because your best player gets tired sometimes.

Champions of the business world and the athletic arena alike know they cannot do it all. If they had limitless energy and time, however, they would undoubtedly be able to handle all issues and circumstances that arise. Many of these champions try, but eventually they do fail. The smart champions learn this lesson early. Even if those delegates who give champions help aren't as gifted in solving the issues, these team members are necessary because of the time and effort they save the champion. Over time delegates experience the same dilemma as champions, and thus a corporation is born.

Anything that seems too good to be true has a great marketing plan behind it.

The business of creating a case for buyers to consider purchases is marketing. The better the case that is built the better the ultimate marketing efforts can be. If one is convinced that something is too good to be true then whatever preceded that something: a speech, an advertisement, a poster, a cold call, must have made a very enticing vision about that something. Otherwise instead of being "*too good to be true*" our instincts would reveal it as "*an obvious crock.*" It is the great marketing effort that has us seeing the former instead of the latter.

106

A trump card is not a trump card unless it's played.

While it may provide a feeling of security to hold onto something you're certain will bring about a desired effect, remember that if that something is never put into play, (i.e., cashed in, revealed, exposed, redeemed, or discussed), it is merely held in earnest and rarely gains interest. If the trump card is not known to those you would play it against, it cannot give you its power: its power simply lies in your mind. Further, when you actually do play this card, it may no longer have the value you considered so dear when you first held it.

107

People do listen when you scream.

Screaming is childish, boorish, annoying, and at work, very embarrassing. Repeated screaming most likely leads to others avoiding you like the plague. But screaming is also intimidating, attention getting, and even more effective at gaining someone's ear than a calm repose. You will remember throughout your life those things that people screamed at you much more than those things people calmly stated to you. The trick about screaming is finding someone to scream at, i.e., someone who hasn't yet run from you.

Caller ID tells us whom we wish to talk to.

Caller ID is simply about control. Everyone can call, few are chosen. Long-distance telemarketers need not apply. Caller ID screens you from the world more than it screens the world from you. The world has at least made an effort to contact you. With Caller ID, you decide whose voice you are willing to tolerate. For those who do brave the telecommunications maze, they win the glory of five seconds of your voice.

109

Most who lead cannot, most who follow shouldn't. So there is balance.

Managerial positions are full of LWB's ("Leader Wannabee's"), who actually believe they are leaders. By some twisted fate of corporate ascension, these LWB's have landed in the chair of Solomon because of factors like tenure, familiarity, and, God help us, attrition. LWB's eventually come to realize they're just not meant for leadership. Still, they keep their mouths shut because doing otherwise would lead to corporate suicide. Conversely, many with vision, charisma, passion, and compassion are overlooked because of their age, humility, or worse, a poisoned reputation, often fueled by LWB's who recognize that individual's true leadership qualities.

110

The purpose of an interview is to DIS-qualify.

Recruiters and hiring managers have to process a litany of information. So many resumes and cover letters to sift through, it's no wonder Hirestoppers ever look at any of them. Thus they practice negativism, discard everything you don't like, and whatever is left, like it. People inevitably are treated the same way by Hirestoppers. While interviewing may expose potential employers to some outstanding candidates, Hirestoppers don't have time to determine why each candidate is worthy. Instead, they look for any and every reason: weight, height, accent, degree, birthplace, or spelling errors, to reject candidates. Unfortunately for job seekers, most interviewers will risk the backlash of disqualifying potentially fantastic candidates.

111

The squeaky wheel gets the grease. Why shouldn't it?

A squeaky wheel is one of the most annoying things in the world. It rarely goes away without some attention, so why not just attend to it and move on? Because it upsets the balance of fairness? What's fair about being continuously bothered or destroying the morale of an entire group because Mr. Squeaky complains incessantly? But if Mr. Squeaky is placated, won't others require equal soothing? The "greasing" law does not support that theory. When all the wheels squeak simultaneously, they are much more likely to be replaced than soothed. Therefore, they police themselves and stop squeaking.

112

Intimidation, though unpopular, is almost always desired.

Sellers of products, services, or ideas have always intimidated buyers by subtly creating fear in them. When a seller wishes to gain the acceptance of their product or idea, the seller creates fear by scaring benefactors with one of the following adages, "What happens if the product is not purchased, the service is not rendered, or the idea is not embraced?" The seller then demonstrates how the purchase will remove those fears. Through considering all the repercussions, mostly negative, if the sale is not made, buyers coerces themselves into purchasing products, services, or ideas. That coercion through fear is intimidation.

113

It takes more effort and more ridicule from others to be a sycophant, which is why it is more rewarding.

Sycophants might appear lazy, discounting hard work for flattery and insincere behavior, but there isn't a harder way to live. How many times a week do you lie in bed at night, worrying about the constant ire of your coworkers? Would you endure others saying despicable things about you and accusing you of shortcomings, true or not? Could you enjoy a reputation of being less than what you are? After all, no one says, "Hey, Mr. Syco is a real kiss-ass, but wow, what a genius!" Instead, it's usually more like, "That Syco is a real kiss-ass. What an insecure person he is!" Mr. Syco, unlike most of us, must always be on his sycophancy game. When he slips and acts like everyone else, he becomes like everyone else and loses all of the accolades that come with being a smooth talker: promotions, easier assignments, longer lunches, etc. Who would want that kind of pressure?

114

No job of any real importance ever required a cover letter to interview for it.

Jobs of real importance in an organization are gained through relationships and notoriety. High-profile people are sought out by organizations for their perceived ability to garner revenues for that organization. Relationship-oriented placements come from those who want to work with others they already trust to be good fits for the requisite organization. Either these people come by direct word of mouth or by indirect word of mouth. The top positions in firms, the ones of great significance are nearly always filled this way. If one is actually sitting down to write a cover letter espousing why one is the next Benjamin Franklin, chances are he isn't interviewing for any position Ben Franklin would want.

115

The fallen athlete is a myth. It is merely a repackaged thug who too has athletic prowess.

Too often, we look myopically at an individual and define the entire person by the few qualities we see. If a person is smart, for example, we might believe they speak well. We hear of one's wealth and assume they drive an expensive car. We see people wearing designer labels and assume they have money. We look at people who are in good shape and figure their lives are just as well organized. Unfortunately, two things skew our understanding of people: 1) we mostly see what others want us to see and 2) we rarely have the means to see everything about anyone. It is fairly certain, however, that over time, the predominant qualities of a person will find their way to the surface and most of us will eventually notice them.

116

The longer you work for someone, the longer they win.

Working in companies is a game. In our capitalistic society, companies set up all sorts of rules related to their game like, "When you will take your turn," usually between 9 and 5, "What you will be doing during your turn," i.e., your job, and the best rule of all, "This is what we will pay you," i.e., your salary. You play—-you conform. So few of us are above the rules. You might rationalize that you are winning the game because you have acquired some game pieces like money, frequent flyer miles, and corporate trinkets. But these came at a price: you have given your time, energy, creativity, and sacrifice for all the other things you could have done with your life.

117

Whoever invented "praise" was the most masterful puppeteer to date.

To maintain control of a population without rewarding it economically, a leader must make the population feel good about the circumstances in which it finds itself. On a singular level, bosses seek to make employees feel good about their jobs when they cannot enhance their positions. By praising an employee, a boss elevates the employee's stature, and the employee feels better about their current circumstances. Further, if the boss makes the employee feel good enough, the employee will likely accept all other circumstances surrounding his or her status quo, such as not being promoted, not receiving a raise, or not getting satisfying assignments. We have been taught that praise itself is a reward. But most people wouldn't care if financial compensation went up while level of praise went down.

118

Cover letters, no matter how well written, are worthless compared to a decent recommendation.

Cover letters can be constructed so well that they can rouse potential employers to consider candidates, even where no opportunity existed. Cover letters can contain the right verbs, nouns and adjectives, to make candidates sound like superheroes. Ultimately, however, a cover letter is written as a way of gaining entrance into an organization. Either the letter does that or it doesn't. Even when cover letters work there is still a great deal of speculation as to whether or not the candidate is what he claims to be. A decent recommendation, however, breaks through the walls of speculation as if they weren't there in the first place. That is why it is so much easier for others to sell candidates than for candidates to sell themselves.

That is a really good idea.
#@*?&!

"Good idea," means "I should have thought of that."

No one wants to feel stupid about anything, yet certainly there are times when we all do. Perhaps we are just ignorant or uninformed. Unless we are totally spiteful, it is easy to understand why we are inclined to praise others for their good ideas. Still there is a part of all of us, a stronger part in some, which wishes we had the idea instead. By not coming up with the idea ourselves, we are left to wonder what it was we failed to recognize, conclude, or consider: something that would surely have brought about the same idea from our lips instead of theirs. Alas, all we can say humbly is "Good idea."

Most of what you see in business is what others have worked very hard to make you see.

Using press clippings, corporate memos, or websites, businesses paint the brightest possible picture for the company's circumstances. When big sales contracts are won the task is easy. When the circumstances are dire, however, company's constituents must see "hope" and that picture is exceedingly difficult to paint. Companies must shelter their constituents from seeing how and why everything occurs in the company. If they didn't two things would occur: 1) there would too much information, making it difficult to decipher it all, and 2) people would gravitate toward the negative information and lose sight of the whole picture. That's why a company's bankruptcy or its drastic change in policy mostly comes as a shock to its employees and the public.

Never tell an executive what he doesn't want to hear.

No executive wants more problems to deal with then he or she already has. Bad news invariably creates more problems, ones that most likely need to be solved. Your announcement of the problem puts the burden on the executive to solve it. As the messenger, you are now associated with the problem. Further, if you have not solved the problem or presented a solution, you will likely be labeled a troublemaker, no matter how much you have been lauded for bringing the message to light.

122

He who lies first is most believed.

We don't expect others to lie about things just for the sake of lying. Normally we banter with rationale where discussions are supported by example or fact. But unprovoked statements carry a credibility they shouldn't have. That's because unprovoked statements cause us to react to them before questioning their validity. By reacting to the statements, we focus more on how to deal with what was said rather than whether or not it is true. When maligned individuals attempt to defend a statement's falseness it's too late: an impression has already been set. It takes a tremendous amount of undoing just to get one's reputation back to where it was when the lie was first perpetrated. Many argue it never returns. That is why huge settlements are made in the cases of celebrities who feel they've been violated or workers who feel unjustly dismissed.

All employees are not equal, though the ideology is novel and convenient.

Under the law, "opportunity" may be equal for all employees, but decision makers within a corporation value no two employees equally. Why should they be? If they were, everyone in the corporation would be able do everyone else's job. Every employee would contribute equally. Every employee would be compensated identically. We know that is never the case. While unpopular to hear it, disparity is easy to believe. Falsely, we have projected the "equal opportunity" thrust to insinuate that everything regarding employment, job transition, job movement, and compensation, is equal for all employees. Decision makers, however, have skillfully found ways around the "equal" thrust whenever they've needed to cater to employees of higher value.

124

The best ideas come from arguments, not from discussions.

Discussions aren't necessarily calm, nor are arguments always violent. By nature, a discussion is the mulling of an idea, perhaps even an idea in depth. However, arguments suggest opposing views of the same point, i.e., competition, and only with opposing views can new views plead their case. Our civil democracy is the foundation of this ideology in America. It's long documented that competition breeds progress and that only by fueling competition will progress continue.

125

COLLEGE:
Convincing Others Long Lasting Education Guarantees Excess

You've heard it before: "Go to college, get a degree, and become successful. Better degree-more success." College's marketing bent is that the odds favor those with advanced degrees reaping greater levels of income. Colleges over-exploit this marketable statistic to attract their customers. Colleges are businesses, just like any other business. Their customers are enrollees, and their product is, among other things, education. To be profitable, colleges must convince their enrollees that what they endow upon them is essential, as would any other business expecting to sell a product. What better way to convince a college's customers than to emphasize the marketability of prosperity? College cannot guarantee one's prosperity, but through the repeated promotion of the "financial success" statistic, prosperity becomes almost a college's promise. Unfortunately, what is promoted is at best "hope." In fact, most of what increases the probability of prosperity happens outside of college, and not in it.

Most people think they think outside of the box.

Not being able to think outside the box connotes a diminutive view of the world. This marks one as a simpleton. Mr. Outabox, as with so many other employees, therefore sees himself as something a little higher on the "omniscience" food chain. Mr. Outabox wears his namesake as a badge of superiority over simpletons but he isn't alone. Many Mr. and Mrs. Outabox employees, in their insistence of being unlike so many simpletons, make themselves exactly like each other. Being an out of box thinker is marked by not thinking like the others. Therefore Mr. and Mrs. Outabox really aren't out of box thinkers.

127

Employees would rather read a blatant lie than hear incontrovertible truth.

The profundity of the written word is that if someone took the time to write it, then it must carry some level of credibility that supersedes what is spoken. We afford publications the benefit of having been researched, and when we read the words, we know they are immortalized. After all, who would spend so much time formatting and reworking and editing a report that isn't true? Ironically, in our age of computers, color laser printers, and the host of text fonts available, publishing the written word is almost as easy as speaking it.

128

Common sense is not another form of intelligence; it's an excuse for the logically challenged.

Common sense defined is "sound practical judgment independent of specialized knowledge or training; normal native intelligence." Webster, for all of his wonders with the English language, is wrong. Sound judgment requires the processing of information, regardless of how spontaneous or rote the judgment appears and how little or great the information processed. And where is the line drawn about whether knowledge is specialized or not? One's lack of common sense is really one's lack of information. Logicians lacking information quickly determine that certain knowledge pieces are missing and they need to be acquired. Conversely, Commonsensors, those who cling to this notion that they have some unique intelligence "gift" when they simply have prescient information, are intelligence-pretenders who have not yet proven themselves logical.

Even inventions can be hurried.

There is a certain mystery surrounding inventions that they take place in small rooms behind closed doors. We have this image of Thomas Edison tinkering in a room alone or masterful entrepreneurs sweating in their basements on their free time. Thus we believe inventions almost happen by chance. This, however, is only one clouded image of invention. So many inventions take place in large rooms or labs with many individuals coerced into coming up with the latest version of a societal panacea. When inventions (saleable products or services) stall, more and more talent and material is brought in until a product or service is created. If inventions can't be hurried, why do companies budget millions of dollars and place timelines on research and development? Companies certainly wouldn't let these departments survive if their ability to create was happenstance.

What is written is always simultaneously fiction and non-fiction.

Writings are fiction simply because the medium of words cannot exactly capture whatever those words are attempting to describe. Even someone as prolific as Thomas Jefferson was a reporter of circumstances, his view of how things were. Words can touch, move, and inspire–but they can only tell a story, not be the story itself. No matter how believable or entertaining the words, they are the product of another's thoughts and not the actual circumstance they attempt to describe. It is non-fiction because the words are real, regardless of whether or not they convey a lie, a story, or one's version of the truth.

Computers have accelerated our rush toward processing competence and thinking incompetence.

Computers are the consummate logicians: they define everything with a one or zero, i.e., a yes or no, an on and off. Our increased use of computers, by staging more and more circumstances and events on them, has spawned new ways of thinking. At the same time, however, we've let these stagings increasingly confine us to handling problems via logical and process-oriented transactions. This rule-based ideology stymies both our willingness and creativity to conceive how the problems of business might be solved differently. We rely on models instead of intuition; spreadsheets instead of facts; spellchecker instead of learning how to spell correctly. As the scales further tip toward solving problems on the computer, we'll eschew what our own brains are capable of in favor of the answers we'll expect to find inside the brain of the computer.

132

The best way to package a lie is to publish it with an italicized signature at the end of it.

We are inundated with quotations in nearly every walk of life. We see them as announcements on television, on the headings of book chapters, and in the reprints of all kinds of speeches. We pay heed to the all-powerful statements and the sages who lent their names to such words of wisdom. After all, who would lend their name to something that isn't true? To support the "truth" the name of the sage is italicized and slick, promoting professionalism and an attention to detail, further solidifying the notion that the point of the sage is true. This is why the movie industry so proudly promotes its upcoming attractions this way. Unfortunately, by the time you realize Joe Critic was full of it and the movie wasn't "The most spectacular display of acting this side of Gone with the Wind," you're still out twenty bucks.

There is just as much if not more creativity in a successful business plan than there is in an architectural feat, an impressionist painting, or a sci-fi cinema.

Art can exist simply for the sake of art. A successful business plan, however, must be much more, as it is worthless without an audience to buy into it. It needs financiers, those willing to front money and buy into the plausibility of the plan. It needs a solution, one creative enough to warrant financing. It requires a steadfast timeline, one that might restrict the creativity of the business plan developer. It has to capture a market, another factor that might restrict the creativity of the business plan developer. A painting has none of these restrictions. Constructing a successful business plan requires us to surge up to or beyond what we naturally expect in artistic creativity.

A good idea is nothing more than that.

Good ideas, like the invention of the personal computer and the fast-food restaurant, while they might lead to wonderful things in our society, are merely seeds spread in an open field. To fruit, those seeds need a champion, someone who sustains their momentum. It's the Mr. Gardeners of the world who set up the distribution channels for the seeds and it is the Mr. Gardeners that ensure the seed can be sold profitably. Sometimes Mr. Gardener is also the manufacturer of the seed. Unfortunately most ideas never find a Mr. Gardener and thus we never find out about the seed.

When isn't somebody using his brain?

If you aren't using your brain, you must be dead. Even if it is just a figure of speech, "not using your brain" has no merit. People don't just stop thinking. They simply haven't figured out what we expected them to, and we're incredulous that they just didn't get it. The reasons prohibiting their cognitive conclusions could reach into the millions. But we'd rather judge them, professing, "It's so clear to me; why don't you understand?"

136

Corporate rumors often have more information than corporate announcements.

In the hierarchy of information authenticity, corporate announcements rest at the top and corporate rumors lie on the bottom. But which one really says more? Announcements undergo intense scrutiny to become publishable for the general population of employees. They're mostly written by individuals specifically hired to disseminate information that favors the overall corporation. Good announcements are easy to deliver; bad announcements must be mitigated to minimize panic. Corporate rumors, on the other hand, have no rules associated with their release. They are rarely edited for carefully chosen words regardless of their newsworthiness. A corporate rumor can be as grand or as bad as the messenger believes it is. Many of the flowery words used to obviate the message in announcements are cast off thus leaving the rumor more direct and informative.

There are two profound truths concerning the written word: 1- that it was written, and 2-that it was thought.

Whether it's the headlines of a newspaper or the crawl across the television, words appear and we take them for granted as being the truth, simply because they were printed. Too often, these words become false over time. When this happens, more headlines appear, or retractions appear on page L-20. The truth of a story is always debatable and often prosecutable. So what are we to believe about the words we read? 1) Words cannot appear without being written, regardless of which medium is used to scribe them and which vehicle carries them; and 2) Words cannot appear without being thought, regardless of who thought them.

138

Most of the time, you don't have to pay for your mistakes.

Push me-pull me. Looking at Newton's third law, it's no wonder we believe everything we do incorrectly will eventually come back and bite us. But does it really? So many times we've erred in our lives, only to go on without penalty. Then when something bad does happen to us, we try to attribute the "payment" to all of our mistakes leading up to it. This is completely unrealistic, for two reasons. First, the payment you've just made could have been for a thousand other reasons than the mistakes you made. Second, mistakes are really not known without hindsight. What may simply appear at one time to be a mistake may eventually reveal itself as a stroke of genius or luck.

139

Succeed at what you dislike and you will forever be condemned to it.

Being very good at something in business can be a blessing if you enjoy doing it. Others regard you as an expert and you gain a glowing reputation. You are continuously consulted for that skill and praised for it. You are locked into the job because now everyone has complete confidence in your abilities and your position. Naturally, everyone thinks you are the happiest employee in the world. But what if you dislike what you do so well? The same thing: Expert-Consultancy-Praise-Lockdown. Why should anyone be concerned with your happiness when you're performing so well? You aren't going anywhere, right? That's just what the company is banking on.

Success breeds success-but a great deal more contempt.

As one goes through one's professional life, patterns of behavior repeat themselves, making one's success or failure rarely a one-time thing. While success breeds itself into more success, unfortunately it also breeds contempt from others. Others openly laud our successes but too often lament their own fate, musing, "Why not me?" This self-pity can only go on for so long before it turns into jealousy, spite, or even anger. The greatest form of contempt for another's success is bitter rationalization: "Sure, she's President of the firm but spends zero time with her family."

141

Good outcomes come more from hindsight than from good planning.

Fail to plan, plan to fail. Blah, blah, blah! Who plans to fail? That's a ridiculous notion. Whatever someone pursues they are pursuing with the notion that they are doing the right things, i.e., what is necessary to create a desired outcome. While one might fail through their efforts the failure is only known in hindsight because no one knows whether someone is going to fail at something until they have, in fact, failed. Too often we've seen victory snatched from the jaws of defeat demonstrating that there is more than one way to succeed at anything. Practice and discipline are heralded as great ways of increasing the probability of a desired outcome. However, both can stem one's success if something else later reveals how success might be gained. Of course that won't be known until the outcome is known.

142

Effort does not equal result.

Working hard-even working smart, as some would like to believe to be the superior "work" method-does not guarantee any result. Effort is only one influence toward determining a result, and can be easily mitigated by many other influences: timing, luck, health, and state of mind, to name a few. While you might expend great energy, you may still fail in both your desired and expected results. Conversely, you might expend little effort and reap results far beyond your expectations. Still, we are taught that expending great effort leads to great results. That's because we want to be able to control results, and effort may be something we can control more than other determining factors.

LOSS: Lack of Sufficient Sales

Sales drive the business. No sales, no business. A business with insufficient levels of sales, regardless of how well the company's back office performs, will show dwindling profits and still go out of business. You can essentially perform poorly in any other area of the business and survive if the sales are good enough. If the sales are not good enough, however, no other area can sustain the company.

Fail purposely and eventually you will slide into utopia.

When you fail at a job, chances are you won't keep the job very long, unless you work for the government. If you give yourself the opportunity to fail each time you get a job you dislike, the odds are you'll eventually land a job you do like. Too often however, we are caught up in the notion that we should not fail at our job because we have to be responsible to the job: to succeed at the job through whatever it takes. Being responsible means working hard and succeeding at the job. Being more responsible, however, is leaving the job for someone else who wants it more. The faster you fail, the faster you will succeed.

145

The world doesn't care what you did in high school, college, or even yesterday: it was too long ago.

Our society's ability to forget yesterday is what gives everyone who is not in jail a second and even third chance. CEOs get to remake failing companies and athletes get to renew themselves the following season. We don't concern ourselves too much with the past because we are too concerned with the present and the future. We are a society of hope; hoping the bad of the past won't happen again and the good of the past will happen again. Because of both foci, we need not concentrate on the past. It is ironic that a society so desirous of good outcomes becomes so enamored with others' present failures. Why else would the tabloids be the hottest selling newspapers in the country?

146

Expending more effort to get a job does not make you any better at doing that job than the person who was handed the job on a silver platter.

Mr. Likely candidate may approach the job search with Herculean efforts, such as fifty phone calls and sixteen interviews. He might even send sixteen subsequent "Thank you" letters. He might even bring more experience and knowledge. But what really makes a person better at doing a job is how well she does that job and can improve in that job. Mr. Likely might bring tenacity to the position but so might Ms. Silver Platter. Further Ms. Silver Platter may have no background in the position but still have the natural abilities to perform the position better than most. Given time, she might exceed what Mr. Likely could have ever hoped to accomplish. It is merely our perception of what is fair that has us discounting the validity of Ms. Silver Platter's candidacy.

147

Higher education increases our chances of reaching higher levels of mediocrity.

Those we deem most successful in business are those who have led an effort to great prosperity. While higher learning opens and expands the mind, it mostly provides a grander level of academic understanding. Few institutions if any teach students how to 1) have guts and take chances in business, 2) employ other people to carry out a vision, 3) be lucky, 4) change the status quo, or 5) look for opportunities where they didn't exist before. Instead, academic institutions position students for a life of attrition through existing business institutions, institutions where you can ascend a hierarchical ladder based upon how well you play by the rules of the organization. In essence, academics teach others how to be soldiers, not leaders. And with more academics, soldiers become better soldiers, not leaders.

148

SUCCESS:
SUCking profitably from the CESSpool of willing sheep.

Business success comes from sales and the management of those sales. Perhaps the company created the market for its goods and services or perhaps the market already existed. Either way, no business achieves success until it can profitably handle its business transactions; i.e. revenue and expenses. To do this profitably, companies must not only find a group to purchase their goods or services, they must convince that group to actually buy them. A company's ability to manipulate the purchasing power of the group is what sets up a company's opportunity to manage its expenses in such a way that it can show a profit.

We want to hear from you!

What was your favorite anti-quote and why?
What has *Lights, Cubicle, Action!* made you think about?
What are you going to do differently now?
Do you have any *Lights'* ideas?

Contact Us Now!

Tell us your favorite quote and why you are better off having read it and you'll receive a free poster displaying your favorite quote from the DocVoc Press that you can proudly display in your office.

You can e-mail us at books@docvoc.com or send your message to:

DocVoc Press
P.O. Box 2458
Reston, VA 20195

DocVoc Enterprises

From the cradle to the grave we are taught to achieve. We then hope that understanding and happiness follow. All too often they do not. Enter DocVoc® Enterprises, a no-nonsense Vocational Consulting firm dedicated to the ideology the *"Just a Job is a Terrible Thing."* America's Vocational Doctor, Anthony A. Cantor, a.k.a. DocVoc®, brings forth a compendium of workshops, articles, and speaking engagements, debunking myths from all walks of life. Through education and humor, DocVoc® Enterprises captures the essence of individuals and corporations then finds that idealistic fit we all so desperately seek.

Visit the DocVoc® website: www.docvoc.com:

- Team and Individual Workshops Available
- Corporate Facilitating and Individual Coaching
- Myth-Debunking Articles
- Sample Anti-Quotes for Upcoming Books
- DocVoc® Enterprises Promotional Materials

If you wish to contract a speaking or workshop engagement with DocVoc Enterprises contact admin@docvoc.com. For any additional copies of current publications or advanced notice of new publications please contact books@docvoc.com or write to DocVoc® Press P.O. Box 2458, Reston VA, 20195
For additional copies of *Lights, Cubicle, Action!*, call 1-800-345-6665, fax: 603-357-2073, or email: orders@pathwaybook.com.
For questions related to *Lights, Cubicle, Action!*, or other DocVoc Press publications email: books@docvoc.com

Other books in the *Lights, Cubicle, Action!* Series soon available from the The DocVoc® Press:
Lights, Camera, Life!: 100+ Sparks for Survival in Life, a.a.cantor, Summer of 2003
Love, Camera, Action!: 100+ Heartstrings for Survival in Relationships, a.a.cantor, Summer of 2003

Other Places to Pick Up *Lights, Cubicle, Action!*
www.pathwaybook.com
www.docvoc.com or email books@docvoc.com
Local bookstores

www.JobRadio.com

"Internet Radio For High-Tech Job Searching"

***JobRadio*, the premier Internet Radio Station, Resume Distribution Network and Corporate Agency Management System, is focused on championing both the Technical Candidate and the Technical Recruiting Agency.**

Founded and designed by Recruiters, Account Managers and Technical Talent, JobRadio.com features a streamlined rich environment, which services Candidates and Agencies up to and beyond their most common needs allowing them:

1. To return to the job seeker, power over the distribution of their resume.
2. To introduce entertainment to the existing dreary job search process.
3. To educate, promote, and critique technical recruiting agencies.
4. To become the global information portal in the recruiting industry.
5. To make a little change in the process.

Logon to* JobRadio.com *and download two free hot new products:

Candidate Utility Program (CUP)

The CUP provides the ability to calculate different job opportunities for specific employment types. Whether your searching for Full-Time, Contract-W2, or Contract-1099, you can calculate your Projected Salary, Employment Hours, Taxes, Social Security, Insurance, etc.

Recruiter Utility Program (RUP)

The RUP provides the ability to calculate different recruiting opportunities, for specific employment types. Whether your recruiting for Permanent Placement, or Contract Placement, you can calculate your Placement Fee + Bonus, Contract Hours, Gross and Net Income, Spread, Burden Rate, etc.

"JobRadio.com...The Voice of the Internet"

About the Author

Anthony Cantor, a.k.a. DocVoc® is a Human Resources Consultant who transitions employees through all walks of professional life. For nearly twenty years he has managed multi-million dollar Human Resource and Finance projects for Fortune 500 companies. He founded DocVoc Enterprises, a compendium of Human Resource and Vocational Products dedicated to idea that "Just a Job is a Terrible Thing." His articles appear on www.docvoc.com, www.Jobradio.com and in several corporate newsletters nationwide. Through his humorous and provocative style his articles answer common questions related to vocational dream pursuit and corporate conflict resolution.

As a Penn State MBA Honor's Graduate he received Master's Degrees in both Organizational Behavior and Marketing. On assignment in Belgium and Norway he managed consulting projects involving "Successful Cultural Transition" and "Organizational Trust." Formerly a Project Manager and Consultant for MCI Communications in Atlanta, Georgia, he managed implementations of Financial, Marketing, and Sales systems, then continued consulting with the Hunter Group, a Baltimore-based Human Resources Training and Consulting firm. While at Hunter, he created their End-User Training Practice that now services Hunter clients worldwide.

Anthony attended the University of Maryland where he majored in Corporate Finance with a minor in Sports Management. With nearly twenty years of corporate and entrepreneurial experience he has had the benefit of observing and participating within nearly one hundred corporate cultures at every professional and executive level.